Friends
are
Forever

Dr. Criswell Freeman

WALNUT GROVE PRESS
NASHVILLE, TN

Friends
are
Forever

Dr. Criswell Freeman

Walnut Grove Press
Nashville, TN 37203

2nd Edition
ISBN 1-58334-136-6

The ideas expressed in this book are not, in all cases, exact quotations, as some have been edited for clarity and brevity. In all cases, the author has attempted to maintain the speaker's original intent. In some cases, material for this book was obtained from secondary sources, primarily print media. While every effort was made to ensure the accuracy of these sources, the accuracy cannot be guaranteed. For additions, deletions, corrections or clarifications in future editions of this text, please write Walnut Grove Press.

Printed in the United States of America
Cover & Page Layout Design by Bart Dawson
Cover Photo: www.corbis.com
1 2 3 4 5 6 7 8 9 10 • 02 03 04 05 06 07 08 09 10

Acknowledgments: The author is indebted to Angela Freeman, Dick and Mary Freeman, Ron Smith, Jim Gallery, and to the creative staff at Walnut Grove Press.

For Angela,
My Best Friend

Table of Contents

Introduction

Emily Dickinson spoke for friends everywhere when she observed, "My friends are my estate." Dickinson understood that friends are among our most treasured possessions. But unlike a bank account or a stock certificate, the value of a true friendship is not denominated in dollars and cents; it is, in fact, beyond measure.

This book celebrates the joys of building and preserving *your* personal estate of lifelong friends. On these pages, you will enjoy friendly advice from a wide range of notable men and women. You'll read quotations about laughter, loyalty, sharing, and trust. You'll be reminded of what it means to aid an ally, to back a backer, or to console a comrade. You may even be inspired to pick up the telephone and get in touch with a long-lost pal. If so, you will have increased two personal fortunes at once. And, take it from Emily Dickinson: That's smart estate planning.

Chapter 1
A Friend Is...

A friend is a present
you give yourself.

—

Robert Louis Stevenson

What is a friend? A thesaurus offers many synonyms: ally, alter ego, chum, companion, coworker, colleague, helper, pal, and partner, to name but a few. Like the people who create them, each friendship is unique. But one thing is certain: Enduring friendship, while difficult to cubbyhole, is easy to recognize. We know it when we see it.

Epicurus wrote, "Of all the things that wisdom provides to make life happy, by far the greatest is friendship." Over two thousand years have passed since the Greek sage offered this observation, but little has changed. Friendships are still among the most sublime of human pleasures.

The following quotations describe, at least in part, what it means to be a friend. If you're interested in acquiring *or* maintaining one of life's greatest possessions, turn the page.

A true friend is the gift of God, and
he only who made hearts can unite them.

—*Robert South*

Friendship is one mind in two bodies.

—*Mencius*

A friend is like a poem.

—*Persian Proverb*

Friends are relatives you make for yourself.

—*Eustache Deschamps*

A true friend will not always agree with you
    but will always be true to your best interests.

—Nicole Beale

Friendship is a strong and habitual inclination
        in two persons to promote the good
            and happiness of one another.

—Eustace Budgell

My best friend is the man who in wishing me well
            wishes it for my sake.

—Aristotle

Friendship is a word the very sight of which
in print makes the heart warm.

—Augustine Birrell

Friendship is a sheltering tree.

— Samuel Taylor Coleridge

True friendship is self-love at secondhand.

—William Hazlitt

True friends...face in the same direction
        toward common projects, interests and goals.

—*C. S. Lewis*

A real friend feels no need to excuse himself
                for some failing.

—*The Lubliner Rabbi*

A friend is one who makes me do my best.

—*Oswald Chambers*

Friends are an aid to the young, to guard
        them from error; to the elderly, to attend
        to their wants; to those in the prime of life,
        to assist them to noble deeds.

—*Aristotle*

The thread of our life would be dark, Heaven knows!
If it were not with friendship and love intertwin'd.

—*Thomas Moore*

One who knows how to show and to accept kindness
will be a friend better than any possession.

—*Sophocles*

My friend is he who will tell me my faults,
in private.

—*Ibn Gabirol*

A faithful friend is the medicine of life.

—*Old Proverb*

Each friend represents a world in us, a world
possibly not born until they arrive, and
it is only by this meeting that a new world is born.

—Anaïs Nin

True friends are the ones who really know you
but love you anyway.

—Edna Buchanan

Life is a chronicle of friendship. Friends create
the world anew each day. Without their loving care,
courage would not suffice to keep hearts strong for life.

—Helen Keller

The balm of life—a kind and faithful friend.

—Mercy Otis Warren

A friend can tell you things
        you don't want to tell yourself.

—*Frances Ward Weller*

She is a friend. She gathers the pieces and
        gives them back to me in all the right order.

—*Toni Morrison*

Acquaintances ask about our outward life;
        friends ask about our inner life.

—*Marie von Ebner-Eschenbach*

Best friend, my wellspring in the wilderness!

—*George Eliot*

Kindness

The theologian Phillips Brooks advised, "Be such a person, and live such a life, that if every person were such as you, and every life a life like yours, this earth would be God's Paradise." One tangible way of making this world a more godly place is to show kindness to your friends and neighbors.

Today, be a little kinder than necessary. Laugh a little more and smile a little more. Offer up a few extra pats on the back and a few extra words of encouragement. As you travel along life's road, sow seeds of kindness whenever you can. And, rest assured: even a single act of kindness has the potential to change a person's day *or* a person's life.

A friend is the hope
of the heart.

—

Ralph Waldo Emerson

Chapter 2
The Art
of Friendship

A friendship can weather
most things in thin soil,
but it needs a little mulch
of letters and phone calls
and silly presents every
so often, just to save it
from drying out completely.

—

Pam Brown

The philosopher William James observed, "Human beings are born into this little span of life, and among the best things that life has to offer are its friendships and intimacies. Yet, humans leave their friendships with no cultivation, letting them grow as they will by the roadside." James understood that when we leave our friendships unattended, the resulting harvest is predictably slim.

Ralph Waldo Emerson advised, "The only way to have a friend is to be one." Emerson realized that a lasting relationship, like a bountiful garden, must be tended with care. In this chapter, we consider the art of cultivating friends. If you take these words to heart, *your* harvest will last a lifetime.

To have a good friend is one of the highest delights
of life; to be a good friend is one of the noblest
and most difficult undertakings.

—*Anonymous*

I am quite sure that no friendship yields its true pleasure
and nobility of nature without frequent
communication, sympathy and service.

—*George E. Woodberry*

Those who cannot give friendship will rarely
receive it and never hold it.

—*Dagobert D. Runes*

Hold a true friend with both hands.

—*African Proverb*

Friends are lost by calling often and calling seldom.

—*Scottish Proverb*

Friendship with oneself is all-important, because
without it one cannot be friends
with anyone else in the world.

—*Eleanor Roosevelt*

Be a friend to thyself, and others will be so too.

—*Thomas Fuller*

Confidence is the foundation of friendship.
If we give it, we will receive it.

—*Harry E. Humphreys, Jr.*

Radiate friendship and it will return sevenfold.

—*B. C. Forbes*

Silences make the real conversations between friends.

—Margaret Lee Runbeck

True friendship comes when silence between
two people is comfortable.

—Dave Tyson Gentry

All the law is fulfilled in one word, even in this;
Thou shalt love thy neighbor as thyself.

—Galatians 5:14 KJV

There is nothing we like to see so much as
the gleam of pleasure in a person's eye when
he feels that we have understood him.

—Don Marquis

Give and take makes good friends.

—Scottish Proverb

Friendship takes time.

—Agnes Repplier

Friendship is a plant which must be often watered.

—Anonymous

Friendship requires great communication.

—Saint Francis de Sales

Go oft to the house of thy friend,
    for weeds choke the unused path.

—Ralph Waldo Emerson

'Tis the privilege of friendship to talk nonsense
and have nonsense respected.

—*Charles Lamb*

If you want to be listened to,
you should put in time listening.

—*Marge Piercy*

Oh the comfort, the inexpressible comfort of feeling
safe with a person; having neither to weigh thoughts
nor measure words but to pour them all out, just as it is,
chaff and grain together, knowing that a faithful hand will
take and sift them, keeping what is worth keeping, and
then, with the breath of kindness, blow the rest away.

—*Marian Evans*

Friendship is the pleasing game of interchanging praise.

—*Oliver Wendell Holmes, Sr.*

Many a friendship—long, loyal, and self-sacrificing—
rested at first upon no thicker a foundation
than a kind word.

—*Frederick W. Faber*

Politeness is an inexpensive way of making friends.

—*William Feather*

Of all the things you wear, your expression
is the most important.

—*Janet Lane*

If we all told what we know of one another,
there would not be four friends in the world.

—*Blaise Pascal*

Treat your friends as you do your pictures,
and place them in their best light.

—*Jennie Jerome Churchill*

Keep the other person's well-being in mind when
you feel an attack of soul-purging truth coming on.

—*Betty White*

The best rule of friendship is to keep your heart
a little softer than your head.

—*Anonymous*

To find a friend one must close one eye.
To keep him—two.

—*Norman Douglas*

When my friends lack an eye, I look at them in profile.

—*Joseph Joubert*

Too late we learn, a man must hold his friend unjudged,
accepted, trusted to the end.

—*John Boyle O'Reilly*

The art of being wise is knowing what to overlook.

—*William James*

To be social is to be forgiving.

—*Robert Frost*

Two persons cannot long be friends if they
      cannot forgive each other's little failings.

—*Jean de la Bruyère*

Friendship flourishes at the fountain of forgiveness.

—*William Arthur Ward*

What I cannot love, I overlook. That is friendship.

—*Anaïs Nin*

Do not save your loving speeches for your friends
   till they are dead; do not write on their tombstones,
      speak them rather now instead.

—Anna Cummins

One who knows how to show and to accept kindness
   will be a friend better than any possession.

—Sophocles

Actions, not words, are the true criteria
   of the attachment of friends.

—George Washington

You can make more friends in two months by becoming
   interested in other people than you can in two years
   by trying to get other people interested in you.

—Dale Carnegie

When befriended, remember it.
When you befriend, forget it.
—*Poor Richard's Almanac*

Don't ask of your friends what you yourself can do.
—*Quintus Ennius*

Cooperation is spelled with two letters: WE.
—*George M. Verity*

He who looks for advantage out of friendship
strips it all of its nobility.

—*Seneca*

Live for thy neighbor if thou wouldst live for thyself.

—*Seneca*

The greatest gift we can give one another is
rapt attention to one another's existence.

—*Sue Atchley Ebaugh*

A friend to everybody and nobody is the same thing.

—*Spanish Proverb*

Friendship, by its very nature, is freer of deceit
than any other relationship.

—*Francine du Plessix Gray*

Loyalty is what we seek in friendship.

—*Cicero*

Friendships, like marriages, are dependent
on avoiding the unforgivable.

—*John D. MacDonald*

You can keep your friends by not giving them away.

—*Mary Pettibone Poole*

Be slow in choosing a friend, slower in changing.

—*Benjamin Franklin*

We awaken in others the same attitude
of mind we hold toward them.

—Elbert Hubbard

We should behave to our friends as we
would wish our friends to behave to us.

—Aristotle

Happiness is achieved only by making others happy.

—Stuart Cloete

Friendship is in loving rather than being loved.

—Robert Seymour Bridges

There can be no friendship when there is no freedom.
Friendship loves the free air and will not be
fenced up in straight and narrow enclosures.

—*William Penn*

Other people are like a mirror which reflects
back on us the kind of image we cast.

—*Bishop Fulton J. Sheen*

Lead the life that will make you kindly and friendly
to everyone about you, and you will be surprised
what a happy life you will live.

—*Charles M. Schwab*

Patience

Friendship requires patience. From time to time, even our most considerate friends may do things that worry us, or confuse us, or anger us. Why? Because they are human. And, because they are human, we must, on occasion, be patient with our friends' short-comings (just as they, too, must be patient with our own).

The next time you find yourself drumming your fingers while waiting for a friend to do the right thing, take a deep breath and remain calm. After all, our friends live—and grow—according to their own timetables. Sometimes, we must wait patiently for them, and that's as it should be. After all, think how patient others have been with us.

The most beautiful discovery true friends make is that they can grow separately without growing apart.

—

Elizabeth Foley

Chapter 3
Trust

No soul is desolate
as long as there is
a human being for whom
it can feel trust
and reverence.

—

George Eliot

The philosopher Cicero wrote, "Loyalty is what we seek in a friendship." He was right. Without loyalty, true friendship is impossible. But, with loyalty, true friendship is inevitable.

Trust is a two-way street. We trust those people who have proven themselves trustworthy. And, if we are to be trusted by others, we, too, must earn their trust.

A lifelong friendship, one that is built upon honesty and loyalty, is a beautiful thing to behold. Through the quotations that follow, we examine the foundation of any friendship worthy of the name. That foundation is trust.

Few delights can equal the mere presence
of one whom we trust utterly.

—*George MacDonald*

A man who doesn't trust himself
can never really trust anyone else.

—*Cardinal de Retz*

Convey thy love to thy friend as an arrow to the mark,
to stick there, not a ball against the wall,
to rebound back to thee.

—*Francis Quarles*

Surely we ought to prize those friends on whose
principles and opinions we may constantly rely.

—*Hannah Farnham Lee*

Trust men and they will trust you; treat them greatly
and they will show themselves great.

—*Ralph Waldo Emerson*

The only way to make a man trustworthy
is to trust him.

—*Henry Stimson*

Trust begets truth.

—*Sir William Gurney Benham*

Confidence is the only bond of friendship.

—*Publilius Syrus*

Nothing wounds a friend like a want
of confidence.

—*Jean Baptiste Lacordaire*

A friend is a person with whom I may
be sincere. Before him, I may think aloud.

—*Ralph Waldo Emerson*

I always felt that the great high privilege, relief, and
comfort of friendship was that
one had to explain nothing.
—*Katherine Mansfield*

You can always tell a true friend: when you make a fool
of yourself he doesn't think you've done
a permanent job.
—*Lawrence J. Peter*

A friend knows how to allow for mere quantity
in your talk, and only replies to the quality.
—*William Dean Howells*

It is a vice to trust all and equally a vice to trust none.

—*Seneca*

Love all, trust a few.

—*William Shakespeare*

Better trust all and be deceived than doubt one heart that,
if believed, had blessed one's life
with true believing.

—*Fanny Kemble*

The man who trusts other men will make
fewer mistakes than he who distrusts them.

—*Camillo Benso*

If it wasn't for trusting,

there would be

no living in this world;

we couldn't even eat hash

with any safety.

—

Josh Billings

Let us move on and step out boldly, though it be
    into the night, and we can scarcely see the way.
        A Higher Intelligence than the mortal
            sees the road before us.

—*Charles B. Newcomb*

A man who trusts nobody is apt to be
        the kind of man nobody trusts.

—*Harold Macmillan*

It is more shameful to distrust our friends
        than to be deceived by them.

—*La Rochefoucauld*

Honesty

From the time we are children, we are taught that honesty is the best policy. But sometimes, it is so hard to be honest and so easy to be less than honest. So, we convince ourselves that it's alright to tell "little white lies." But there's a problem: Little white lies tend to grow up, and when they do, they cause havoc and pain in our lives.

Sometime soon, perhaps even today, you will be tempted to sow the seeds of deception, perhaps in the form of a "harmless" white lie. Resist that temptation. Truth is the right way, and a lie—of whatever color—is not.

Virtue is its own reward.

—

John Dryden

Chapter 4
Old Friends

There is only one thing
better than making
a new friend, and that
is keeping an old one.

—

Elmer G. Leterman

It has been said that the best mirror is an old friend. But, a lifelong pal is more than a mirror; he or she is also a priceless treasure.

Thomas Edison said, "I have friends whose friendship I would not swap for the favor of all the kings of the world." All of us know how Edison felt. New friends are wonderful, of course, but they can't take the place of old ones, not even if the new acquaintances are kings or queens!

If you have an old friend you haven't called in a while, why not pick up the telephone today? The call won't cost much, and your friend will be thrilled to hear from you. Besides, the king probably has an unlisted number.

Ah, how good it feels! The hand of an old friend.
—*Henry Wadsworth Longfellow*

Old friends are the great blessing of one's later years.
They have a memory of the same events and
have the same mode of thinking.
—*Horace Walpole*

As in the case of wines that improve with age,
the oldest friendships ought to be
the most delightful.
—*Cicero*

Real friendship is a slow grower.

—*Lord Chesterfield*

The companions of our childhood always possess
a certain power over our minds.

—*Mary Wollstonecraft Shelley*

There is a magic in the memory of a schoolboy
friendship. It softens the heart and even affects
the nervous system of those who have no heart.

—*Benjamin Disraeli*

There's no friend like someone who has known you
since you were five.

—*Anne Stevenson*

Years and years of happiness only make us realize how
lucky we are to have friends who have shared and
made that happiness a reality.

—*Robert E. Frederick*

When you are young and without success,
you have only a few friends. Then, later on,
when you are rich and famous, you still have a few…
if you are lucky.

—*Pablo Picasso*

It is one of the blessings of old friends that
you can afford to be stupid with them.

—*Ralph Waldo Emerson*

Friendship is a spiritual thing. It is independent of matter
or space or time. That which I love in my friend is not
that which I see. What influences me in my friend
is not his body, but his spirit.

—*John Drummond*

Staying Connected

Old friends. We know that we should stay in touch, but there's so little time...and we're so busy. No matter. As loyal friends, we must take the time and make the effort to stay connected.

This very day, someone you know needs a word of encouragement, or a pat on the back, or a helping hand, or a heartfelt prayer. And, if you don't reach out to your trusted friends, who will? If you don't take the time to understand their needs who will? If you don't stay in touch, why should they? So, today, look up an old friend, pick up the phone, and start dialing. It's easy to stay connected with old friends...and oh so rewarding.

Old friends are best
unless you catch a
new one fit to make
an old one out of.

—

Sarah Orne Jewett

Chapter 5
A Helping Hand

What we freely give,

forever is our own.

—

George Granville

The philosopher Seneca wrote, "Wherever there is a human being, there is an opportunity for kindness." How true. We, like Seneca, are faced with countless opportunities to lend a helping hand. May we all take full advantage of those opportunities.

Today, make this pledge to yourself and keep it: be a cheerful, generous, courageous giver. Someone very near to you needs a helping hand, and the hand that helps might as well be yours. Do whatever you can as soon as you can. And, "as soon as you can" means "now."

Fortify yourself with a flock of friends!
You can select them at random, write to one,
dine with one, visit one, or take your problems to one.
There is always at least one who will understand, inspire,
and give you the lift you need at the time.

—*George Matthew Adams*

Everyone needs help from everyone.

—*Bertolt Brecht*

No person was ever honored for what he received.
Honor has been the reward
for what he gave.

—*Calvin Coolidge*

What is serving God? 'Tis doing good to man.

—*Poor Richard's Almanac*

When you cease to make a contribution,
you begin to die.

—*Eleanor Roosevelt*

Goodwill to others helps build you up.
It is good for your body.
It is the real elixir of life.

—*Prentice Mulford*

The smallest actual good is better than the
most magnificent promise of impossibilities.

—*Macaulay*

Even if it's a little thing, do something for those
who have need of help, something for which
you get no pay but the privilege of doing it.

—*Albert Schweitzer*

We cannot hold a torch to light another's
        path without brightening our own.

—Ben Sweetland

Give what you have. To someone else
        it may be better than you dare to think.

—Henry Wadsworth Longfellow

Find out how much God has given you and
        from it take what you need; the remainder
        is needed by others.

—Saint Augustine

Live and let live is not enough;
        live and help live is not too much.

—Orison Swett Marden

When a person is down in the world,
an ounce of help is better than
a pound of preaching.

—*Edward Bulwer-Lytton*

An ounce of help is worth a pound of pity.

—*Old Saying*

Time and money spent in helping men to do more
for themselves is far better than mere giving.

—*Henry Ford*

The truest help we can render an afflicted
man is not to take his burden from him,
but to call out his best energy, that he
may be able to bear the burden.

—*Phillips Brooks*

It takes wisdom and discernment to minister
　　　　to people in need. We must look beyond
　　　　the apparent and seek to meet the needs
　　　　　　of the whole person.

　　　　　　　　　　　　　　—Richard C. Chewning

The only gift is a portion of thyself.

　　　　　　　　　　　　　　—Ralph Waldo Emerson

I hate the giving of the hand unless the
　　　　whole man accompanies it.

　　　　　　　　　　　　　　—Ralph Waldo Emerson

We cannot live only for ourselves.
A thousand fibers connect us with our fellow men.

—*Herman Melville*

The service we render others is the rent
we pay for our room on earth.

—*Sir Wilfred Grenfell*

To give pleasure to a single heart by a single kind act is
better than a thousand head-bowings in prayer.

—*Saadi*

I wonder why it is that we are not all kinder to each other.
How much the world needs it! How easily it is done!

—*Henry Drummond*

All altruism springs from putting yourself
in the other person's place.

—*Harry Emerson Fosdick*

In the time we have, it is surely our duty
to do all the good we can to all the people
we can in all the ways we can.

—*William Barclay*

I expect to pass through life but once. If, therefore,
there be any kindness I can show, or any good thing
I can do for any fellow being, let me do it now,
as I shall not pass this way again.

—*William Penn*

Help your brother's boat across,
and your own will reach the shore.

—*Hindu Proverb*

The greatest good you can do for another is not just to share your riches, but to reveal to him his own.

—

Benjamin Disraeli

We are cold to others only when
we are dull in ourselves.

—William Hazlitt

Friendship is not a fruit for enjoyment only,
but also an opportunity for service.

—Greek Proverb

We secure our friends not by accepting favors
but by doing them.

—Thucydides

Make yourself necessary to somebody.

—Ralph Waldo Emerson

Encouragement

Part of the art of friendship is learning the skill of encouraging others. And make no mistake: encouragement is a skill that is learned over time and improved with constant use. How, we ask, can we be most encouraging? The answer is found, in part, by reminding ourselves what genuine encouragement is and what it is not.

The dictionary defines encouragement as, "the act of inspiring courage and confidence." Genuine encouragement is not idle flattery nor is it pity. It is instead the transfer of courage from one person to another. It is a firm reminder of the other person's talents, strengths, resources and opportunities. Encouragement is confidence shared...and multiplied.

To pull a friend
out of the mire,
don't hesitate
to get dirty.

—

Ba'al Shem Tov

Chapter 6
The Joy
of Giving

An act of goodness
is of itself an act
of happiness.

—

Maurice Maeterlinck

Any way you slice it, generosity is the icing on the cake of friendship. We human beings invest untold energy in the ancient and respected art of giving, and we do so for a very good reason: A thoughtful gift always enriches the giver as well as the recipient.

The Renaissance philosopher Erasmus wrote, "He does himself good who does good to his friend." Do yourself a favor and do one for a friend. Big-hearted giving is the surest way to have your cake and eat it too.

Every charitable act is a stepping-stone toward heaven.

—*Henry Ward Beecher*

We make a living by what we get,
    but we make a life by what we give.

—*Norman MacEwan*

Without kindness, there can be no true joy.

—*Thomas Carlyle*

There is no happiness in having or in getting,
    but only in giving.

—*Henry Drummond*

It is enough that I am of value to somebody today.

—*Hugh Prather*

It is more blessed to give than to receive.

—*Acts 20:35 NIV*

Friends are angels who lift our feet when our
own wings have trouble remembering how to fly.

Anonymous

So long as you can sweeten another's pain,
life is not in vain.

—*Helen Keller*

Happiness consists in giving and in serving others.

—*Henry Drummond*

An unshared life is not living.
He who shares does not lessen, but greatens, his life.

——Stephen S. Wise

Provision for others is a fundamental
responsibility of human life.

—Woodrow Wilson

God loveth a cheerful giver.

—II Corinthians 9:7 KJV

He who does not live in some degree
for others, hardly lives for himself.

—Michel de Montaigne

A man wrapped up in himself makes
a very small bundle.

—Benjamin Franklin

Cheerful Giving

The Bible reminds us that it is more blessed to give than to receive. In other words, those of us who give of our time and our resources are even more blessed than those who receive our gifts. And, because we are blessed when we give, we should do so gladly.

Today and every day, let us give cheerfully. Let us celebrate life with smiles on our faces, kind words on our lips, and songs in our hearts. Let us be generous with our praise and free with our encouragement. And then, when we have celebrated life to the full, let us invite others to do likewise. After all, this is God's day, and He has given us clear instructions for its use. We are commanded to rejoice, to be generous, and to be glad. So, with no further ado, let the celebration begin...

In about the same
degree as you are
helpful, you will
be happy.

—

Karl Reiland

Chapter 7
The Pleasures
of Friendship

Shared joys make
a friend.

—

Friedrich Nietzsche

The French essayist and aviator Antoine de Saint-Exupéry wrote, "There is no hope or joy except in human relations." Anyone who has experienced friendship in full bloom knows this statement to be true. Our friends and loved ones provide some of life's greatest delights, but the pleasures of friendship are never delivered on a one-way street. In order to gain happiness, we must first give it away.

Lord Chesterfield observed, "Pleasure is reciprocal; no one feels it who does not at the same time give it. To be pleased, one must please." In this chapter, we examine the two-way pleasures of friendship.

Friendship is the source of the greatest pleasures, and
without friends even the most agreeable
pursuits become tedious.

—*Saint Thomas Aquinas*

A sympathetic friend can be quite as dear as a brother.

—*Homer*

Just thinking about a friend makes you want to do
a happy dance, because a friend is someone
who loves you in spite of your faults.

—*Charles Schulz*

Friendship ought to be a gratuitous joy,
like the joys afforded by art.

—*Simone Weil*

Arise, and eat bread, and let thine heart be merry.

—*I Kings 21:7 KJV*

One cannot have too large a party.
A large party secures its own amusement.

—*Jane Austen*

The best times in life are made a thousand times
better when shared with a dear friend.

—*Luci Swindoll*

Happiness to me is enjoying my friends and family.

—*Reba McEntire*

You meet your friend, your face brightens—
you have struck gold.

—*Kassia*

I have learned that to have a good friend is the purest
of all God's gifts, for it is a love that
has no exchange of payment.

—*Frances Farmer*

To get the full value of a joy you must have
somebody to divide it with.

—*Mark Twain*

I feel the need of friendly discourse. I cannot
miss this without feeling, as does any other intelligent
man, a void and a deep need.

—Vincent van Gogh

True happiness arises from the enjoyment
of one's self and from the friendship and
conversation of a few select companions.

—Joseph Addison

A single conversation across the table with
a wise man is worth a month's study of books.

—Chinese Proverb

Friendship is one of the sweetest joys of life.
Many might have failed beneath the bitterness
of their trial had they not found a friend.

—Charles Spurgeon

Good company and good discourse
          are the very sinews of virtue.

—Izaak Walton

The infectiously joyous men and women are those
          who forget themselves in thinking about others
                    and serving others.

—Robert J. McCracken

Cheerful company shortens the miles.

—German Proverb

It's not good to be alone—even in Paradise.

—Old Saying

Enduring Friendship

John Calvin observed, "There is not one blade of grass, there is no color in this world that is not intended to make us rejoice." He might have added that enduring friendships are also intended to cause rejoicing and celebration. But, sometimes, rejoicing is the last thing on our minds. Sometimes, we fall prey to worry, frustration, anxiety, or sheer exhaustion…and our hearts become heavy. What's needed is plenty of rest, a large dose of perspective, a heaping helping of faith, and the encouraging words of a trusted friend…but not necessarily in that order.

The real friend is he
or she who can share
all our sorrow and
double our joys.

—

B. C. Forbes

Chapter 8
Laughing
with Friends

Happiness is not perfected until it is shared.

—

Jane Porter

F ew sounds on earth can compare with the music of friends laughing together. Hearty laughter is oil in the engine of friendship: With laughter, things run smoothly; without it, the gears have a tendency to grind.

Arnold Glasow observed, "A loyal friend laughs at your jokes when they're not so good and sympathizes with your problems when they're not so bad." Herein, we consider the joys of a good laugh and the blessings of a good friend with whom to share it.

Laughter moves your internal organs around.
It is an igniter of great expectations.

—Norman Cousins

It is often just as sacred to laugh as it is to pray.

—Chuck Swindoll

For me, a hearty "belly laugh" is one
of the most beautiful sounds in the world.

—Bennett Cerf

Laugh, and the world laughs with you.

—Ella Wheeler Wilcox

There is no man that imparteth his joys to his friends,
but he joyeth the more.

—*Francis Bacon*

Nobody who is afraid of laughing, and heartily too,
at his friend can be said to have a true and
thorough love for him.

—*Julius Charles Hare*

You grow up the day you have
your first real laugh at yourself.

—*Ethel Barrymore*

Learning to laugh at ourselves,
we did not lack for things to laugh about.

—*Michael Ramsey, Archbishop of Canterbury*

A cheerful friend is like a sunny day,
　　which sheds its brightness on all around.

—*John Lubbock*

Laughter is the sun that drives winter from
　　　　the human face.

—*Victor Hugo*

Wear a smile and have friends; wear a scowl
　　　and have wrinkles.

—*George Eliot*

The clearest sign of wisdom is continued cheerfulness.

—*Michel de Montaigne*

"Live to love" was my father's motto.
"Live to laugh" is mine.

—*Hannah Cowley*

A friend is someone who can see through you
but still enjoys the show.

—*Farmers' Almanac*

Laughter can be more satisfying than honor;
more precious than money;
more heart-cleansing than prayer.

—*Harriet Rochlin*

God hath made me to laugh,
so that all that hear will laugh with me.

—*Genesis 21:6 KJV*

A good laugh is sunshine in a house.

—*William Makepeace Thackeray*

The most thoroughly wasted of all days
is that on which one has not laughed.

—*Chamfort*

Friendship improves happiness and abates misery
by doubling our joy and dividing our grief.

—*Joseph Addison*

Among those whom I like or admire,
I can find no common denominator,
but among those whom I love, I can:
All of them make me laugh.

—*W. H. Auden*

The first day I gave a laugh, my tears were
blown out like candles. It takes effort to push back the
stone from the mouth of the tomb.

—Mary Lavin

All who would win joy must share it;
happiness was born a twin.

—Lord Byron

Unshared joy is an unlit candle.

—Spanish Proverb

Laughter dulls the sharpest pain and flattens out
the greatest stress. To share it is to
give a gift of health….

—Barbara Johnson

A man isn't poor if he can still laugh.

—Raymond Hitchcock

The time to be happy is now. The way to be happy is to make others so.

—Robert Ingersoll

The best way to cheer yourself up is to cheer up somebody else.

—Mark Twain

And Let Me Laugh

Lord, when I begin to take myself or my life too seriously, let me laugh.

When I rush from place to place, slow me down, Lord. Give me Your perspective, Your wisdom, and Your peace. And let me laugh.

When the day is cloudy, keep me mindful that above the clouds, the sun still shines. And let me laugh.

And, each morning, when I open my eyes to a world of glorious possibilities, let me give thanks for the gift of life. Then, let me rise up and make the most of that gift. Let me strive toward a worthy purpose, and let me celebrate each day with a song, and a smile, and a prayer…and, let me laugh.

Amen

Laughter is the shortest
distance between
two people.

—

Victor Borge

Chapter 9
Friendship in
Tough Times

There is no greater
loan than a
sympathetic ear.

—

Frank Tyger

Plato advised, "Be kind, for everyone you meet is fighting a hard battle." He might have added that sometimes the battle rages so fiercely that we must call in the reserves. Trusted friends are the reserve troops who help us survive and conquer the inevitable skirmishes of life.

Ovid observed, "As the yellow gold is tried in fire, so the faith of friendship must be seen in adversity." If you have an acquaintance who is being tested by fire, volunteer your services today. Who knows? Your support might just turn the tide of battle.

No man can be happy without a friend
    nor be sure of his friend till he is unhappy.
                      —Thomas Fuller

The firmest friendships have been formed in mutual
    adversity, as iron is most strongly united
        by the fiercest flame.
                      —Charles Caleb Colton

It is not so much our friends' help that helps us,
    as the confidence of their help.
                      —Epicurus

Don't walk in front of me, I may not follow.
    Don't walk behind me, I may not lead.
    Walk beside me and just be my friend.
                      —Albert Camus

Real friendship is shown in times of trouble;
    prosperity is full of friends.

—*Euripides*

Prosperity makes friends; adversity tries them.

—*Publilius Syrus*

Prosperity is not a just scale; adversity is
    the only balance to weigh friends.

—*Plutarch*

When true friends meet in adverse hour;
    'tis like a sunbeam through a shower.

—*Sir Walter Scott*

In prosperity our friends know us;
in adversity we know our friends.

—John Churton Collins

The shifts of fortune test the reliability of friends.

—Cicero

Friendship makes prosperity more brilliant
and lightens adversity by dividing and sharing it.

—Cicero

Trouble shared is trouble halved.

—Dorothy Sayers

A friend in need is a friend indeed.

—*Old Saying*

A friend should bear his friend's infirmities.

—*William Shakespeare*

Sad things aren't the same as depressing things.

—*Thornton Wilder*

There are times when God asks nothing of his children except silence, patience and tears.

—*C. S. Robinson*

Friendship, of itself a holy tie, is made
more sacred by adversity.

—*John Dryden*

Trouble is a sieve through which we sift our
acquaintances. Those too big to pass through
are our friends.

—*Arlene Francis*

We long to find someone who has been where
we've been, who shares our fragile skies,
who sees our sunsets with the same shades of blue.

—*Beth Moore*

No matter what happens to you, if you can draw
strength from God and the people you love,
nothing can ever defeat you.

—*Reba McEntire*

In poverty and other misfortunes of life,
true friends are a sure refuge.

—Aristotle

But every road is tough to me that has
no friend to cheer it.

—Elizabeth Shane

The friend of my adversity I shall always cherish most.
I can better trust those who helped to relieve
the gloom of my dark hours than those who
are so ready to enjoy with me the sunshine
of my prosperity.

—Ulysses S. Grant

Do not protect yourself by a fence but
rather by your friends.

—Czechoslovakian Proverb

Friendship is one of the sweetest joys of life.
Many might have failed beneath the bitterness
of their trial had they not found a friend.

—*Charles Spurgeon*

The hearts that never lean must fall.

—*Emily Dickinson*

The meek become known in anger, the hero in war,
and a friend in time of need.

—*Ibn Gabirol*

The true way to soften one's troubles
is to solace those of others.

—*Madame de Maintenon*

A cheer for the noble breast
That fears not danger's post;
And like the lifeboat, proves a friend,
When friends are wanted most.

—*Eliza Cook*

Adversity

Throughout the seasons of life, all of us, on occasion, endure losses that leave us breathless. Sometimes, of course, it is not we but instead our friends who face adversity. When they do, our mission is simple: We must assist in any way we can, either with an encouraging word, a helping hand, or a heartfelt prayer.

The English clergyman Charles Kingsley had this practical advice: "Make it a rule, and pray to God to help you to keep it, never, if possible, to lie down at night without being able to say: 'I have made one human being at least a little wiser, or a little happier, or at least a little better this day.'" Amen to that… especially when times are tough.

When a friend is in trouble, don't annoy him by asking if there is anything you can do. Think up something appropriate and do it.

—

Edgar Watson Howe

Chapter 10
All-Purpose
Advice

The best time to make
friends is before
you need them.

—

Ethel Barrymore

Advice is easy to give and harder to take. Edna St. Vincent Millay wrote to a friend requesting, "Please give me some good advice in your next letter. I promise not to take it." We all know the feeling.

On the following pages, we offer a potpourri of wisdom worth taking, no matter what your friends say.

Friendship was given by nature to be an assistant
to virtue, not a companion in vice.

—Cicero

He that walketh with wise men shall be wise.

—Solomon

Friendship with the upright is profitable.

—Confucius

Do not remove a fly from your friend's
forehead with a hatchet.

—Chinese Proverb

If the world is cold, make it your business
to build fires.

—*Horace Traubel*

Be slow to fall into friendship; but when thou art in,
continue firm and constant.

—*Socrates*

Blessed are they who have the gift of making friends
for it is one of God's best gifts. It involves many
things, but above all the power of loving
out of one's self and appreciating whatever
is noble and loving in another.

—*Thomas Hughes*

Don't bypass the potential for meaningful friendships
just because of differences. Explore them.
Embrace them. Love them.

—*Luci Swindoll*

It is wise to pour the oil of refined politeness
on the mechanism of friendship.

—*Colette*

If two friends ask you to judge a dispute, don't accept,
because you will lose one friend; on the other hand,
if two strangers come with the same request,
accept, because you will gain one friend.

—*Saint Augustine*

Friendship is seldom lasting but between equals,
    or where the superiority on one side is reduced
      by some equivalent advantage on the other.

—Samuel Johnson

Have no friends not equal to yourself.

—Confucius

The most called-upon prerequisite of a friend
      is an accessible ear.

—Maya Angelou

Avoid fried foods, hard liquor, and negative people.

—Marie T. Freeman

A word of kindness is seldom spoken in vain,
>   while witty sayings are as easily lost
>   as the pearls slipping from a broken string.
>   —*George Prentice*

Seek those who find your road agreeable,
>   your personality and mind stimulating,
>   your philosophy acceptable, and your
>   experiences helpful. Let those who do not
>   seek their own kind.
>   —*Henri Fabre*

Never claim as a right what you can ask as a favor.
>   —*John Churton Collins*

Since there is nothing so well worth having
>   as friends, never lose a chance to make them.
>   —*Francesco Guicciardini*

Friends are those rare people who ask how we are
and then wait to hear the answer.

—*Ed Cunningham*

To be pleased, one must please.

—*Lord Chesterfield*

Never miss an opportunity to say a word
of congratulations.

—*Lyndon Baines Johnson*

Surround yourself with people who believe in you.

—*Brian Koslow*

Often we can help each other most by leaving
each other alone; at other times we need
the handgrasp and the word of cheer.
—*Elbert Hubbard*

The worst solitude is to be destitute of sincere friendship.
—*Francis Bacon*

When someone does something good,
applaud! You'll make two people happy.
—*Samuel Goldwyn*

Nothing is ever lost by courtesy. It is the cheapest of
pleasures, costs nothing, and conveys much.
It pleases him who gives and receives and thus,
like mercy, is twice blessed.
—*Erastus Wiman*

Charm is simply this: the Golden Rule, good manners,
good grooming, good humor, good sense,
good habits, and a good outlook.

—Loretta Young

Friendship that flames goes out in a flash.

—Thomas Fuller

It is the peculiar quality of a fool to perceive
the faults of others and to forget his own.

—Cicero

Hate the sin and love the sinner.

—Mahandas Gandhi

The true secret of giving advice is to be perfectly
indifferent whether it is taken or not.
—*Hannah Whitall Smith*

Never explain—your friends do not need it,
and your enemies will not believe you anyway.
—*Elbert Hubbard*

The man who thinks he can live without others
is mistaken; the one who thinks others
can't live without him is even more deluded.
—*Hasidic Saying*

Tell me thy company, and I'll tell thee what thou art.

—Miguel de Cervantes

The wise man seeks a friend with qualities
which he himself lacks.

—Jeremy Taylor

Associate yourself with men of good quality
if you esteem your own reputation, for
'tis better to be alone than in bad company.

—George Washington

"Stay" is a charming
word in a friend's
vocabulary.

—

Louisa May Alcott

The familiar words of 1st Corinthians 13 remind us that love is a priceless gift indeed. Faith is important, of course. So too is hope. But love is more important still. Today, let us spread the gift of love to friends and family...by word and by example. And the greatest of these, of course, is example.

But now faith, hope, love, abide these three; but the greatest of these is love.

—

1 Corinthians 13:13 NASB

Live so that your
friends can defend you,
but never have to.

—

Arnold Glasow

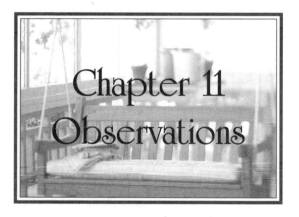

Chapter 11
Observations

Friendship begins
with gratitude.

—

George Eliot

Wherever you are, it is your friends
who make your world.

William James

Robbing life of friendship is like robbing
the world of the sun.

—*Cicero*

Life is partly what we make it and partly
what is made by the friends we choose.

—*Chinese Proverb*

There is no wilderness like a life without friends.

—*Baltasar Gracián*

Friendship is not quick to burn.

—*May Sarton*

I have three chairs in my house; one for solitude,
two for friendship, and three for society.

—*Henry David Thoreau*

There are three types of friends: some are like food—
indispensable; some are like medicine—
good occasionally; and some are like poison—
to be avoided always.

—*Ibn Gabirol*

Constant use will not wear ragged the fabric
of friendship.

—*Dorothy Parker*

Friends—real friends—reserve nothing.

—*Euripides*

By friendship you mean the greatest love,
the greatest usefulness, the most noble sufferings,
the severest truth, the heartiest counsel, and
the greatest union of minds of which brave men
and women are capable.

—*Jeremy Taylor*

There are only two people who can tell you
the truth about yourself—an enemy who has lost
his temper and a friend who loves you dearly.

—*Antisthenes*

Good friends, good books and a sleepy conscience:
This is the ideal life.

—*Mark Twain*

Never while I keep my senses shall I compare anything
to the delight of a friend.

—Horace

The worst solitude is to be destitute of sincere friendship.

—Francis Bacon

Without wearing any mask that we are conscious of,
we have a special face for each friend.

—Oliver Wendell Holmes, Sr.

Friendship has splendors that love knows not.

—Mariama Bâ

That friendship will not continue to the end
which is begun for an end.

—Francis Quarles

Friendship is the only cement that will ever hold
the world together.

—Woodrow Wilson

The reward of friendship is itself. The man who hopes
for anything else does not understand
what true friendship is.

—Saint Alfred of Rievaulx

Friendship is always a sweet responsibility,
never an opportunity.

—Kahlil Gibran

Friendship is almost always the union
of a part of one mind with a part of another.

—*George Santayana*

Perhaps the most delightful friendships are those
in which there is much agreement,
much disputation, and yet more
personal liking.

—*George Eliot*

Animals are such agreeable friends—they
ask no questions, they pass no criticisms.

—*George Eliot*

Old friends are a
comfort to the heart.
Like a favorite robe and
a familiar song, they wrap
you in the warmth of
their presence and you
understand all the words.

—

Pat Matuszak

Friendships,
like geraniums,
bloom in kitchens.

—

Blanche H. Gelfant

We cannot tell the precise moment when friendship
is formed. As in filling a vessel drop by drop,
there is at last a drop which makes it run over.
So in a series of kindnesses there is, at last,
one which makes the heart run over.

—*James Boswell*

Every organism requires an environment of friends,
partly to shield it from violent changes, and
partly to supply it with its wants.

—*Alfred North Whitehead*

You could have been born in another time and another
place, but God determined to "people" your life
with these particular friends.

—*Joni Eareckson Tada*

Duty towards God is to be happy;
      duty towards a neighbor is to give him
      pleasure and alleviate his pain.

—*W. H. Auden*

To be capable of steady friendship or lasting
      love are the two greatest proofs, not only of
      goodness of heart, but of strength of mind.

—*William Hazlitt*

True friends don't spend time gazing into
      each other's eyes. They show great tenderness toward
      each other, but they face in the same direction—
      toward common projects, interests, goals—
      above all, toward a common Lord.

—*C. S. Lewis*

Friends are the family we choose for ourselves.

—*Edna Buchanan*

A man cannot be said to succeed in this life
who does not satisfy one friend.

—*Henry David Thoreau*

Think where man's glory most begins and ends,
And say my glory was I had such friends.

—*W. B. Yeats*

One thing everybody in the world wants and
needs is friendliness.

—William E. Holler

The really serious things in life are earning
one's living and loving one's neighbor.

—W. H. Auden

Age doesn't protect you from love. But love,
to some extent, protects you from age.

—Jeanne Moreau

Nobody, but nobody, can make it out here alone.

—Maya Angelou

To associate with other like-minded people in small
purposeful groups is for the great majority of men
and women a source of profound
psychological satisfaction.

—*Aldous Huxley*

No one person can possibly combine all the elements
supposed to make up what everyone means
by friendship.

—*Francis Marion Crawford*

If you want an accounting of your worth,
count your friends.

—*Merry Browne*

Friendship is the garden of God— what a delight to tend his planting.

—

Inez Bell Ley

The Power of Words

Think…pause…then speak: How wise is the man or woman who can communicate in this way. But all too often, in the rush to have ourselves heard, we speak first and think later…with unfortunate results.

If we seek to be a source of encouragement to friends and family, then we must measure our words carefully. Words are important: they can hurt or heal. Words can uplift us or discourage us, and reckless words, spoken in haste, cannot be erased.

Today, seek to encourage all who cross your path. Measure your words carefully. Speak wisely, not impulsively. Use words of kindness and praise, not words of anger or derision. Remember that you have the power to heal others or to injure them, to lift others up or to hold them back. When you lift them up, your wisdom will bring healing and comfort to a world that needs both.

True eloquence
consists in saying all
that is proper and
nothing more.

—

François de la Rochefoucauld

About the Author

Criswell Freeman is a Doctor of Clinical Psychology living in Nashville, Tennessee. He is the author of *When Life Throws You a Curveball, Hit It* and numerous books in the Wisdom Series published by WALNUT GROVE PRESS.

His Wisdom Books chronicle memorable quotations in an easy-to-read style. The series provides many inspiring, thoughtful and humorous messages from entertainers, athletes, scientists, politicians, clerics, writers and renegades. Combining his passion for quotations with extensive training in psychology, Freeman revisits timeless themes such as perseverance, courage, love, forgiveness and faith.

Dr. Freeman is also the host of *Wisdom Made in America*, a nationally syndicated radio program.